Your Employment Rights

in a week

HILTON CATT AND PAT SCUDAMORE

Hodder & Stoughton

A MEMBER OF THE HODDER HEADLINE GROUP

As the champion of management, the
Chartered Management Institute shapes and
supports the managers of tomorrow. By sharing
intelligent insights and setting standards in
management development, the Institute helps
to deliver results in a dynamic world.

chartered

management

institute

inspiring leaders

For more information call 01536 204222 or visit www.managers.org.uk

Orders: please contact Bookpoint Ltd, 130 Milton Park, Abingdon, Oxon
OX14 4SB.
Telephone: (44) 01235 400414, Fax: (44) 01235 400454. Lines are open from
9.00–6.00, Monday to Saturday, with a 24 hour message answering service.
Email address: orders@bookpoint.co.uk

British Library Cataloguing in Publication Data
A catalogue record for this title is available from The British Library

ISBN 0 340 849142

First published   2002
Impression number   10 9 8 7 6 5 4 3 2 1
Year   2007 2006 2005 2004 2003 2002

Typeset by SX Composing DTP, Rayleigh, Essex.
Printed in Great Britain for Hodder & Stoughton Educational, a division of
Hodder Headline Plc, 338 Euston Road, London NW1 3BH by
Cox & Wyman Ltd, Reading, Berkshire.

C O N T E N T S

In a world ruled by uncertainty and change, knowing your employment rights is more important to you than it has ever been. Added to this, an increasing number of people work on short-term contracts, part-time, in small firms or based at home, i.e. where access to information on rights may be difficult or where employers themselves may have only limited knowledge. So, welcome to this *In a Week* crash course. Over the next 7 days you will be learning where you stand when it comes to addressing all of those difficult job issues, what the law says and where it is on your side. The benefits for you will be:

- Knowing what you are entitled to and what your employer is expected to provide
- Knowing how far you can go when it comes to sticking up for your rights
- Knowing when your employer may be overstepping the mark
- Being one step ahead of unscrupulous employers (the kind who try to pull the wool over your eyes)
- Knowing your rights when your firm is sold out or taken over
- Knowing where you stand when you are asked to change roles or accept new conditions
- Being clued up on your rights if you work part-time or on short-term/temporary assignments
- Knowing your rights if your job comes under threat (when the next round of redundancies is heading your way)

Before you start

Today you will be learning about your pre-employment rights – the rights you have before you start a job. The list of topics is as follows:

- *Discrimination*: Where race, gender or disabilities is the reason that you do not get the job; where selection procedures are not just unfair but also unlawful
- *References*: What rights you have when a prospective employer asks you for a reference; what you can do when something is said about you that is misleading or untrue
- *Medical reports*: What rights you have when an offer of employment is conditional on a satisfactory report from a doctor; the right you have to see the report and challenge its contents
- *Criminal convictions*: How far an employer can go into your background; where you stand if you think some past misdemeanour has put paid to your chances
- *Prying questions*: What rights you have when prospective employers want to probe into your private life
- *Misrepresentation by employers*: The duty employers have to not give you false information about a job
- *Offers that are withdrawn*: Where you stand if a job offer is cancelled

Discrimination

In deciding who gets the job and who does not, it is unlawful for employers to discriminate against applicants because they are the wrong gender or race or because of their disabilities. There are a few exceptions to this rule. For example, a film company when casting for a part can stipulate actors of a certain sex and/or ethnic origin that is consistent with the character they are going to play.

These so-called genuine occupational qualifications are, however, rare and are unlikely to be found in most normal mainstream employment.

Race
Race discrimination extends to colour, race, nationality or national or ethnic origin. This means it is just as taboo to turn down applicants because they are Welsh as it is to say no to them because they are black or they are Eskimos.

Sex
Sex discrimination includes discrimination on grounds of marital status as well as gender. So, for example, it is unlawful to give preference to a single person because the job involves long stays away from home, i.e. married people might have more problems adjusting. Refusing employment to a woman because she is pregnant is quite clearly sex discrimination (the less favourable treatment is linked directly to her sex).

Disabilities
Turning an applicant down because he or she has a disability is also unlawful unless the employer considers first whether it would be possible to make an adjustment to the job. For

instance, if the job involves working in an environment where fumes are present and the applicant has a chest condition, the employer could look at how practical it is to provide a face mask.

Disability has a wider meaning under the 1995 Disability Discrimination Act than it did previously. A disability is defined as any physical or mental impairment that has a 'substantial and long term adverse effect on [the] ability to carry out normal day-to-day activities'. The bottom line here is that any employer who turns you down for a medical reason is potentially treading on thin ice.

Direct and indirect discrimination
Race and sex discrimination are broken down into two types – *direct* and *indirect*.

- At the selection stage, *direct discrimination* arises when interview lists and short-lists are drawn up or job offers are made to exclude candidates of a particular sex or racial group
- *Indirect discrimination* is rather more subtle. It can happen, for example, when a selection criteria is used which makes it harder for members of a particular sex or racial group to qualify

References

A common enough event when you are applying for a job is to be asked to give the name of a referee. Having observed the usual formalities of checking with the referee first to see if he or she is happy to act on your behalf, you are then usually left in the dark as to what actually goes in the reference. If you do not get the job, your thoughts naturally turn to the reference and whether the referee said something about you that served to put your prospective new employer off.

So what are your rights when it comes to references?

Exercising care
In most cases the reference in question will be from a previous employer, for example, your boss in your last or most recent job. Incumbent on such a person is a duty to take reasonable care over what goes in the reference; Notably that:

- Any information is accurate
- Any opinions stated are based on accurate facts

What this means in practice is that if you did not get the job because of a bad reference and if the information supplied in the reference was untrue or misleading, then you could have a case for claiming damages. Your ex-employer did not exercise care and you have a right to expect this.

Libel

The law also protects you if anything said in a reference is libellous, i.e. if your ex-employer really oversteps the mark and makes a statement about you that is an unjustified slur on your character.

Because of legal challenges, employers are getting more and more wary about what they put in written references or they resort to only giving references over the phone. Does the law give you any protection against false, misleading or slanderous verbal references? The answer is yes. The difficulty is, of course, proving what has been said.

The right to see a reference

The first challenge you face when taking issue with an unfavourable reference is getting sight of it so that you can check what it says. Some employers may be prepared to show you the references they have received but the majority – not wishing to get drawn into arguments – will probably say no. Is there anything you can do to force an employer to show you a reference? The answer is yes. If an unfavourable reference is given as the reason you are not offered a job and

you suspect it contains false or misleading information, you can go to a court and ask for the reference to be disclosed.

Warning

Before exercising this right, bear in mind that a referee is perfectly at liberty to give a fair and well-founded opinion of you even though it may not be to your liking. In other words, do not go down this route simply because of sour grapes. Reserve action for those who, out of carelessness or maliciousness, have scuppered your chances of getting a job you deserve.

Medical reports

A job could be offered to you subject to a medical report and in this instance the report could be one supplied by your doctor or by a company-nominated practitioner. What are your rights when it comes to medical reports? Do you have the rights to:

- See what the medical report says?
- Challenge it if you feel it is misleading or wrong?

The right to say no
Of course it could be that you object to a medical report as a matter of principle. It has to be said that a report can only be submitted to an employer with your written consent. However, withholding consent could create an impasse as far as moving your application forward is concerned. This is an avenue you should only go down after careful consideration of the likely repercussions.

The right to access
You have the right to see any medical report before it is shown to an employer or alternatively you can ask to see any report that has been submitted in the last 6 months. The latter is useful if, for example, you chose not to see the report before it was submitted but you subsequently found yourself turned down for the job because the report was unsatisfactory. You may be intrigued to discover what the report had to say and you can exercise your right by making a request to the doctor who supplied it.

Challenging a medical report
You can challenge a medical report if you feel that it is
misleading or wrong and you can do this by writing to the
doctor who supplied the report, giving your reasons. The
doctor then has two choices:

- If the doctor accepts what you are saying he or she
  can amend the report
- If the doctor disagrees with you then he or she can
  send in the report in its original form and you have
  the right to attach a statement saying why you
  consider the report to be misleading or wrong.

You have a further right in these situations and that is to refuse
permission for the report to be passed on. Again, however, this
is a case of first considering the likely repercussions.

Criminal convictions

When you apply for a job it is normal practice to be asked to
fill in an application form on which you may be asked to
declare any criminal convictions. Equally the question 'Do you
have any criminal convictions?' may crop up during the
course of an interview. So where do you stand when
employers seek to make enquiries into the murkier parts of
your past? How far can they pry and what rights do you have?

'Spent' convictions
You do not have to disclose any conviction that is 'spent'.
This term is used by the Rehabilitation of Offenders Act 1974
to define the point at which your debt to society is repaid and
the slate is wiped clean. 'Rehabilitation periods' as they are

known, depend on the type of sentence received. For example, the rehabilitation period for a fine is 5 years.

If a prospective employer asks you to declare any convictions and if your convictions are spent then the proper answer to give is 'none'. If a spent conviction subsequently comes to light (i.e. during the course of your employment) the law continues to protect you. For example, if an employer dismisses you for concealing a conviction that is spent, the dismissal would automatically be unfair and you could claim compensation.

'Prying' questions

What other protection does the law afford you when it comes to questions at interviews or on application forms – questions that do not seem to have any bearing on your ability to do the job? What, for example, if a prospective employer asks you intimate questions about your sex life or to disclose information about your political views?

Sensitive personal data
There are certain categories of information which are defined as 'sensitive' under the 1998 Data Protection Act. These are:

- Information about racial or ethnic origins
- Political views
- Religious beliefs
- Trade union affiliations
- Medical information
- Sex life and sexual orientation

- Involvement in crime – including any current criminal proceedings

If you are asked to disclose sensitive personal information you have a right to know:

- For what purpose the information is required
- Who will have access to it

It is an employer's duty to ensure that sensitive information is not held on file for any longer than is absolutely necessary.

Some lines of questioning are quite clearly unacceptable. For instance, an employer who asks a female applicant repeat questions about whether she has plans to start a family, is signalling an intention to discriminate on grounds of sex. The answer? If you are turned down for the job, seek redress under the Sex Discrimination Act of 1975.

Unless properly justified, prying questions can also be in breach of your rights under Article 8 of the European Convention on Human Rights – the right to respect the privacy of your home and family life. More of this on Wednesday.

Misrepresentation by employers

Next on the list of pre-employment rights is the right to be given fair and accurate information about the job you are applying for. Where do you stand, for example, if an employer feeds you with false facts at an interview or paints a rose-coloured picture of the job? Furthermore, what if promises are made to you that do not materialise, such as promises to increase your pay after a probationary period or to include you in a bonus plan? Worse still, what if you leave a perfectly good job to take up an offer that has been misrepresented to you?

The law
The Misrepresentation Act 1967 gives you the right to claim damages for any losses you sustain because the terms of a contract have been misrepresented to you and this includes the terms of a contract of employment. What this highlights, of course, is the all-important rule when it comes to job offers – get as much in writing as you possibly can. This especially applies to anything that has a material bearing on your decision to take the job – such as a golden hello or your participation in a share option scheme or a seat on the board at some point in the future. With the terms set out in black and white, there is less scope for argument over whether the job was misrepresented to you or not.

Offers that are withdrawn

You are all set to start in a new job when a letter arrives in the post telling you that everything has changed and that the job is no longer available. Where do you go from here? Is it just a case of gritting your teeth or do you have any rights that you can fall back on?

The contractual position
Tomorrow we will take a look at contracts of employment and one interesting fact will emerge: a contract is formed once an offer of employment is accepted. This means that, when an offer you have accepted is withdrawn, the employer is put in the position of having to terminate the contract –

meaning, in turn, that they have to give you notice. Where, for example, the contract provides for 3 months' notice and you are told that the job is no longer available, then the monetary equivalent of 3 months' notice is owed to you.

Summary

Today we have considered the rights you have when you are applying for a job and going through the various stages of selection. You have learnt that:

- Turning you down because of your race, gender or disabilities is illegal
- Making it harder for you to meet selection criteria for the same reasons is also illegal
- You have recourse to justice if an inaccurate, misleading or libellous reference is the reason that you do not get the job
- You have the right to see medical reports and take issue with what they say
- You have the right to draw the veil over criminal offences that date from a long time ago
- At interviews, you have a right to know the reasons for questions about your private life
- You can retaliate when employers break their promises or do not give you the full facts about a job
- You have the right to compensation if you accept an offer then find that it is withdrawn

Knowing where you stand

Your programme for today looks like this:

- Statutory and contractual rights: know the difference between the two
- Your contract of employment and what it consists of: express and implied terms
- Written particulars
- Job offers, company handbooks and other documents
- Collective agreements
- The spoken word
- Contractual breaches and how they arise
- Remedies

Statutory and contractual rights

Your job rights split into:

- *Statutory rights* – rights everyone has by law
- *Contractual rights* – rights contained in your contract of employment

Statutory rights

Statutory rights have mushroomed in the last 30 years. This partly reflects a greater tendency for governments to legislate on employment rights and partly reflects the influence of the EU (European Union). New rights are coming along all the time and one of the effects of this deluge is that employers are finding it harder and harder to keep up with developments. Small wonder that some of them feel that they are managing in a legal minefield.

Note: you cannot waive a statutory right. It is still there irrespective of any document to the contrary that you may have signed.

Contractual rights
Contractual rights can apply to all employees of an organisation.

• *Example:* The right to join an occupational pension scheme after the completion of a certain period of service.

Alternatively they may only apply selectively to certain groups or individuals.

• *Example:* The right of senior management staff to have a particular grade of company car or the right to a pay increase after 6 months that you negotiated for yourself when you took the job.

Statutory and contractual rights are sometimes at variance. Take notice periods as an example. Your contractual notice period in a job may be 1 calendar month whereas, if you have worked continuously for the same employer for the last 7 years, your statutory entitlement under the Employment Rights Act is 7 weeks. The answer here? Take the greater of the two. In the example we have given the statutory period is greater, therefore it takes precedence.

What is a contract of employment?

Given that your contractual rights are those conferred on you by your contract of employment, what exactly is a contract of employment? What does it consist of and, if you want to check out what it says, where do you look?

Common misunderstandings
Though some employers go into volumes of small print to set out their various rules and conditions, the term 'contract of employment' has a rather wider meaning than the contents of any particular document or set of documents.

Express and implied terms
A contract of employment sets out what the parties to an employment relationship (i.e. the employer and the employee) agree to. In some cases what is agreed is *express*, i.e. uttered by word of mouth or, more commonly these days, set out in writing. In other cases, the terms are implied, i.e. there are no words but there is a common understanding that the term applies.

- *Express terms*: Are usually contained in documents, such as written particulars, job offers, company handbooks, notices displayed on notice boards, documents describing pay arrangements and so forth.
- *Implied terms*: Not only include the law of the land that employers and employees alike must adhere to, but also common custom and practice arrangements and accepted modes of conduct, and so on. Note that the right to reasonable care by your employer when it comes to health and safety matters is an example of an implied contractual term.

Written particulars

Within 2 months of starting a job, you have a right to receive a written statement from your employer covering the main terms of your employment. These written statements provide a useful summary of your more important contractual rights, including pay arrangements, holiday entitlements and pension rights, etc. Alternatively your employer can refer you to documents where this information can be found.

Job offers

Job offers vary enormously in the amount of detail that they contain but usually they will contain confirmation of your job title, salary and principal perks. If there is any promise to review your salary after a period, then a job offer would be the normal place to make mention of this. Otherwise the job offer may simply refer you to other documents for enlightenment (e.g. a company handbook).

Company handbooks

Given various names such as 'Staff Rules' or 'Terms and Conditions of Employment', company handbooks are usually the main source of information on contractual employment rights and are well worth taking the trouble to read carefully.

Other documents
In their extent and detail these vary:

- From employer to employer
- Depending on the nature and seniority of the appointment

For example, among 'other documents' there could be a booklet describing the company pension scheme or arrangements for company car users. More senior appointments could call for you to sign a separate service agreement in which all sorts of rules and obligations are specified.

Collective agreements
Collective agreements are agreements between employers and trade unions which, in some cases, are incorporated into individuals' contracts. The right to an enhanced redundancy payment is an example of the kind of right that is often found in a collective agreement.

Note: where a collective agreement applies to you, your attention should be drawn to it in your statement of particulars (see above).

The spoken word
Express terms do not need to be set out in writing. Indeed, other than the written particulars, there is no obligation on an employer to put anything in writing. However, in practice, 'all oral' contracts tend to be confined to the fringes of the job market, for example, casual work.

Contractual inconsistencies

This is worth mentioning. Occasionally you find that your job rights are set out differently in the different documents you receive from an employer or that what is put in writing is at odds with what has been said at the interviews. An example we heard recently was of an engineer who was told at his interview that he would have a holiday entitlement of 30 days. When the job offer came through it quoted a holiday entitlement of 25 days. What to do in this situation? Get it sorted out immediately. Get the employer to confirm in writing which version is correct. The additional point to make here is to always read the small print of job offers carefully.

> Taken collectively, these various documents and oral statements make up the express part of your contract of employment.

Breaches of contract

A contract of employment:

- Comes into force once an offer is made and it has been accepted
- Is legally binding for both parties
- Cannot be varied except by mutual agreement
- Can only be terminated by giving notice (the period of notice specified in the contract)

If you are denied a contractual right, for instance, if your employer refuses to include you in a bonus scheme despite an undertaking in your letter of appointment, then your employer is technically in breach of the contract. This means that, if necessary, you can go to law to:

- Restore your right
- Recoup any damages

However, where do you stand if your employer seeks to make changes to your contract? What, for example, if you are asked to take a pay cut or if one of your perks is taken away from you, such as your company car?

Your employer may be forced into draconian actions such as these by, say, a slump in the market. Getting you and others to forfeit some of your pay and perks may be the only way of keeping the firm from going under. Nevertheless, however dire the circumstances, your employer must still seek your agreement before making changes to your contract. In short, what your employer cannot do is *impose* a change unilaterally and, if this happens, it would be a contractual breach. Of course, what you have to weigh up in these cases is what the likely repercussions would be if you said 'No'. Your employer may, for example, be left with no option other than to terminate your contract. Advice? Always try and see where your employer is coming from and then negotiate the best deal you can.

Constructive dismissal
But what if a contractual breach forces you into resigning? Where an employer commits a contractual breach and when the result of that contractual breach is that an employee feels that he or she has no option other than to leave, then the path

Warning

A contract of employment can be entered into illegally, for example, where an employer agrees to pay an employee 'cash in hand' without the proper deductions for tax and national insurance. Actions brought for breach of an illegal contract are unlikely to be successful. The moral? Do not dabble in the black economy and, if you do, do not expect any sympathy if it all goes wrong.

is open for that person to seek compensation for constructive dismissal, even though strictly speaking no dismissal has taken place. Claims of constructive dismissal are heard by Employment Tribunals.

Remedies

With employment rights, the usual remedy open to you is to take your case to an Employment Tribunal or, with some contractual rights, to go to a county court. Pause at this point, however, for it goes without saying that starting proceedings against your employer is not going to enamour them to you so it is not a decision that you should ever take lightly.

The lawyer's playground
Going back to what we said at the start of today, the glut of employment legislation in recent years has created a climate of litigation or, as some employers would see it, more and more people are jumping on the bandwagon to put in claims. Coupled with this, the field of employment rights is fast becoming a lawyer's playground where reputations are made and fat fees are earned.

Litigation risks
Apart from putting the relationship with your employer in jeopardy, embarking on litigation carries others risks. Indeed, few of us need reminding that complex lawsuits can be costly and, where no one else is offering to pick up the bill, you

need to be careful. Of course, some law firms offer to work on a 'no win, no fee' basis but here you need to check the small print carefully. The slice that can come out of your hard earned winnings can be frightening!

Talk to your employer
Few employers set out to infringe employment rights intentionally. What is far more likely is:

- Employers who are unaware of their obligations
- Employers whose actions are dictated by the sheer pace of events, i.e. in their hurry to deal with an issue or to get things done they overlook some aspect of individual rights

Given a general willingness on the part of most employers to 'do things right', it is not usually necessary to go to the law to get your rights restored.

Talk to your employer first. Regard going to law as an action of last rather than first resort.

There is a further point to this piece of advice. Courts and Employment Tribunals may take a dim view if they feel that you have not made a reasonable attempt to sort the matter out with your employer first. They may reduce the amount of any compensation they award to you or, in extreme cases, they may strike your claim out altogether or order you to pay costs.

Is it serious?
A further question you need to ask yourself before flying off to see your solicitor: 'Is the denial of my rights something

serious or is it trivial and something I can live with?' For example, if out of general sloppiness and inefficiency, your employer fails to give you a written statement of employment particulars, do you haul the company before an Employment Tribunal or do you let the matter lie? Here, arguably, the denial of your right is having little effect on your day-to-day life. If employment conditions are reasonably well documented elsewhere, then going to a tribunal would seem to serve little purpose other than establishing a point of principle.

Where litigation is justified
However, if the infringement of your rights is not trivial and if your efforts to bring reason to prevail by talking to your employer have not worked, then litigation could be the only course of action left open to you. Fears over how your employer will react will not arise if you have been dismissed or if an infringement of your rights has brought about your resignation. But, if retaliation is a concern, note you have a right not to be victimised if you challenge your employer on an infringement of your rights. An employer who does this would have to answer to an Employment Tribunal for his or her actions.

Where to get help
People can and do represent themselves in Employment Tribunals but, with the increasing complexity of employment law, this may not be in your best interests. If the matter is a fairly simple one – for instance, your ex-employer has failed to give you the correct period of notice – then you may be able to go along and plead your own case. If, however, large sums of money are involved or complicated issues are at stake (e.g. the breach of an executive contract) then legal representation may be advisable.

Where to go from here is very much a matter of personal preference. Most large law firms have one or more employment specialist and, as part of the service and before you spend too much money, they will give you an opinion on your chances of success. Where cash is a constraint, there is a network of Citizens Advice Bureaux across the UK who will be able to help you put together a case. Alternatively, they may be able to put you in touch with a free law service that operates in your area. If you are a member of a trade union, legal representation may be one of the benefits available to you. ACAS (the government's Advisory Conciliation and Arbitration Service) has a duty to see if claims can be settled before they reach a tribunal. Their number is in the phone book and you can seek their advice in confidence before you put in a claim. You will always get an honest and impartial opinion from ACAS, providing that you tell them all the facts and leave nothing out.

Where the issue is race, gender or disability discrimination, you can speak to the government-appointed commission with responsibility for promoting better standards. These are:

- *Race*: Commission for Racial Equality.
- *Gender*: Equal Opportunities Commission.
- *Disabilities*: Disability Rights Commission.

In some (more serious) cases or where an issue of legal principle is at stake, these commissions may even be prepared to back you.

Summary

Today we have looked at how your rights are made up:

- Statutory rights – rights you have by law
- Contractual rights – rights you have as a consequence of your employment

We have seen:

- How employers are not always aware of your rights but, once reminded, they usually take the correct action
- How legal redress is available if an employer attempts to ride roughshod over your rights, but you should always view the law as your weapon of last resort (only to be used if all else fails)

Pay

Money is arguably the main reason most of us go out to work, but what are our rights when it comes to pay? Today we are going to look at:

- A fair day's pay and what rights you have
- Bonuses, allowances and expenses – where you stand when your entitlements are disputed
- Deductions from pay – what your employer can and can not do
- Pay cuts – when your employer asks you to take a drop in earnings
- Equal pay – where gender could be the reason you are being paid less
- Your right to be paid for holidays
- Salary when you are off sick, laid off, on maternity or suspended

A fair day's pay

Where exactly do you stand when you feel your employer is not paying you enough? Do you have a right to a decent wage or is it simply a case of looking for another job?

Minimum pay
As far as statute law is concerned, the only constraint on your employer is to pay the National Minimum Wage. However, since this is a very basic figure aimed at protecting the low paid, it does not provide much in the way of assistance for many people.

Nevertheless, before dismissing the subject of minimum pay altogether it is useful to bear in mind that some industries and organisations have their own minimum wage, often set out in collective agreements (agreements between employers and trade unions). In other words, you may have a *contractual* entitlement to a minimum wage and this could be worth looking into.

Incremental scales

These are worth mentioning because, whether you know it or not, your salary may be subject to an incremental scale. That is, a scale by which your salary goes up periodically in line with, say, your age or the length of your service.

Incremental scales are often included or referred to in the documents that come with your job offer. Alternatively, they may be contained in annual pay statements or collective agreements.

> If your salary is subject to an incremental scale, then your progression up the scale is a contractual right.

Pay review

You may not be subject to an incremental scale (most people are not). Instead, you may rely on periodic reviews of your salary, for example, annually. So where do you stand if your salary is not reviewed or the rise you get is not to your liking?

You may be in the position where there is nothing in your contractual terms to say that your salary will be reviewed. A starting salary may be quoted in your job offer, but nothing is mentioned about what happens afterwards. Where do you stand? If your salary has stayed the same for a number of

years then clearly, at some stage, you are going to start to feel the pinch.

While the absence of any firm commitment to review your salary periodically is not very helpful, if you find yourself in this predicament, you are not as marooned as you may think. For instance, you could argue that, as an *implied* term of your contract, your employer is obliged to make adjustments to your salary occasionally and failure to do so amounts to a contractual breach. Someone who quits because their salary has been frozen for many years, probably has good grounds for a claim of constructive dismissal.

No pay rise

Even where there is an express contractual right to a periodic pay review, it is not necessarily a guarantee that you are going to get anything. Indeed, if you are on the receiving end of a zero increase, it could be your just deserts for a lacklustre performance or simply that your employer does not have the cash to splash out on pay rises. However, if the zero increases go on year after year, then there is an argument that the right to some kind of rise is an implied term.

Pay rise not enough

Here we are entering into the world of subjective judgements where 'enough' is not something that you can measure easily against the yardstick of contractual rights. Where there is clearly a breach, however, is if you have been promised a rise and, for one reason or another, the rise is not forthcoming or is only paid in part. Another possible contractual breach is when everyone on your grade is given a bigger rise than you. It could be argued that your implied right is to the general level of increase.

Bonuses, allowances and expenses

What rights do you have when it comes to other money items in your package? Where do you stand when you are at loggerheads with your employer over payment?

Some employers seek to give themselves flexibility with bonuses by inserting the word 'discretionary' at appropriate places in the rules of the scheme. Here, your contractual right to payment may rest on how the discretion has been exercised in the past. If, for example, the bonus has been in place for many years, its sudden disappearance could still be viewed as a contractual breach.

Bonuses

When part of your salary is paid as a bonus or commission, the rules governing its payment form part of your contract. This means that:

- Failure to pay the bonus (or to pay only a portion of it) is a contractual breach
- Similarly, failure to pay the bonus on the date it is due is also a contractual breach
- Cancelling the bonus altogether falls under the same heading
- Varying the rules can only be done with your agreement (see Monday's unit)

Allowances
Under this heading are items such as luncheon allowances, city weightings, night out allowances, etc. Again, these form part of your contract so, like bonuses, any tampering could constitute a contractual breach.

Expenses
You have a right in law to be paid for any expenses that you incur on your employer's business. This extends to items such as:

- Travel and subsistence expenses
- Purchases of any materials you need to do your job

Deductions from pay

Where do you stand if your employer decides to take a slice out of your salary? What rights do you have if you find some of the money that you have earned has been siphoned off for some reason?

What the law says about deductions
The Employment Rights Act 1996 protects you if your employer attempts to deduct money from your pay and, if necessary, you can go to an Employment Tribunal to ask for the missing amount to be restored. There are, however, some

deductions that employers are allowed to make and these fall
into three categories:

- Deductions required by law
- Deductions that are provided for in your contract of
  employment
- Deductions that you have agreed to

You have a right in law to an itemised pay statement
setting out any deductions. From this itemised
statement you can quickly see if any illegal deductions
are being made.

Examples of illegal deductions are:
- 'Fining' employees for bad work
- Recouping the cost of damage to materials or
  equipment
- Making good an overpayment of expenses
- Taking back money advanced as a loan (except
  where authorised)

In all of the above examples the employee's agreement to the deduction must be sought first, i.e. before the deduction is made.

Pay cuts

What if a pay cut is forced on you because of some redefinition of your job responsibilities? What if your employer asks you to take less money to help the firm through hard times?

What does your contract say?
Your employer's right to vary what you are paid is governed by your contract of employment. Therefore, you need to check through all the documents that you have been given to see whether there is anything that gives your employer the freedom to adjust your pay in certain circumstances or in response to certain events. Since, in most cases, you will find that your contract of employment is silent on these matters, the only way your employer can lawfully introduce a pay cut is by:

- *Either*: getting your agreement
- *Or*: terminating your contract and offering you a new one

With the second of these two options, providing you have got more than 12 months' service, you can, if you are unhappy, say no to the offer and claim unfair dismissal

> Remember that if you are forced to quit because your employer imposes a pay cut on you, you can claim constructive dismissal.

(more on unfair dismissal on Saturday).

Equal pay

What if you are a woman and you feel that your poor pay is because of your sex? What if your male colleagues are earning more than you?

The Equal Pay Act 1970 gave women the right to be paid the same as men for:

- The same or similar work
- Work of equal responsibility

Where men and women work alongside one another doing exactly the same job, the meaning of equal pay is clear enough. It gets a little more difficult, however, where occupations are one sex, for example, the clerical staff of the Accounts office is entirely female. Here the answer might be to draw comparisons with male clerical workers employed elsewhere in the organisation. Is there a gaping differential? If so, and if there is no other justification, there could be an equal pay issue.

Payment for holidays

What right do you have to paid holidays?

Statutory rights
Except in the first year of your employment when different rules apply, you have the right under the Working Time Regulations 1998 to a minimum of 4 weeks' paid annual leave.

Note: all public or bank holidays are included in the calculation of this minimum entitlement.

Contractual entitlement
The chances are, however, that your *contractual* entitlement (the paid holiday entitlement given to you by your employer) is greater than the statutory entitlement.

Other pay rights

Off sick
Once you have been off work for 3 days – and subject to certain rules – you have the right to receive Statutory Sick Pay (SSP) for a period of 28 weeks. Again, however, it is likely that you will also have a *contractual* entitlement to sick

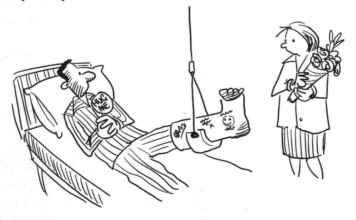

pay and this entitlement will be described in your company handbook or terms and conditions of employment. In most cases this will mean that you will get full salary for a period of time followed by perhaps a further period at a lower rate (employers' arrangements vary quite widely). Here it is normal practice for SSP to be offset against contractual payments, i.e. contractual payment + SSP = normal salary.

Laid off
Where do you stand with regard to pay when you are laid off. If, for example, your employer has no work for you to do or when an external event, such as a power cut or a strike at a key supplier, forces your employer to send you home?

There is a statutory guarantee payment – a fixed amount your employer must pay you on days when you are laid off without any work. However, this guarantee payment is:

- A very basic figure
- Only payable for 5 work-less days in any 3-month period

Collective agreements often have clauses dealing with pay during lay-offs and, if your conditions are subject to collective agreements, then this is a good place to look to find out about your rights. Failing this, it could be a question of going through your company handbook and other documentation to see what your contract of employment has to say about lay-offs. Do not be too surprised if you do not find anything – particularly if you are in a salaried occupation. The subject is frequently left out – either because your employer does not foresee any circumstance in which you would have to be laid off or simply because it has not occurred to them. The difficulty is one they then have to face. If they have to lay you off and do not pay you, there is nothing in your contract to say they can do this. This means that you (and any of your colleagues in the same situation) can go to the law and ask for your pay to be restored.

On maternity

If you take maternity leave you have the statutory right to receive maternity pay from you employer. To qualify for maternity pay you must give your employer proper notice of your intention to take leave and provide medical evidence of the date when your baby is due.

Some employers have arrangements for maternity pay that go far beyond the basic statutory provision.

Suspension

Suspension (being instructed to stay at home and not to come to work) can come under one of two headings:

- Suspension on medical grounds
- Suspension for disciplinary reasons

Suspension on medical grounds most commonly arises when your employer has concerns that your continued attendance at work could impair your health. You may feel you are perfectly fit to be there but your employer may insist on playing safe.

Providing that you have been employed for at least 1 month, the Employment Rights Act 1996 gives you the right to be paid your full normal salary if you are suspended from work on medical grounds.

Suspension for disciplinary reasons is usually aimed at:

- Exacting a punishment on you for a disciplinary offence that you have committed

- Hitting you in the pocket by suspending you without pay so that you will think twice before committing the same offence again

Your contract of employment determines whether or not your employer can suspend you without pay for disciplinary reasons. If there is no provision, then your employer could be committing a contractual breach. But check before kicking up a fuss. The alternative could be dismissing you – particularly if you have had previous warnings or if the offence is serious.

Summary

Today we have explained the rights that you have when it comes to pay. You have seen how the law:

- Protects against unscrupulous employers who tamper with your pay and make up their own rules
- Lays down a framework of minimum entitlements with which all employers must comply

The right to fair treatment

There are standards of behaviour that all employers have to conform to and today we shall look at these. The list of topics is as follows:

- Equal opportunities
- Victimisation, harassment and bullying – the right to be protected from abuse and extreme forms of conduct
- The right to join or refuse to join a trade union
- The right to a fair hearing
- Human rights – the European Convention and how it affects you
- Rights of part-timers, people on temporary contracts, agency workers and freelancers

Equal opportunities

What if you feel that your career is not advancing in the way that it should? What if you feel that you are getting a raw deal when it comes to training and promotion opportunities? What if you think that the reason for your less favourable treatment is your race, gender or disabilities?

Sex discrimination
Women frequently get exasperated with what they see as a 'glass ceiling' over their heads, when it comes to promotions. The jobs are there, but for some reason they seem to be reserved for men.

On Sunday we saw how the law protects job applicants from being discriminated because of their gender. This protection continues after employment begins and it is unlawful to restrict training and promotion opportunities to one sex or, for that matter, to provide benefits or facilities on a one sex only basis.

Though overt or direct sex discrimination in employment is rare, discrimination in its more subtle or indirect form is ingrained into the fabric of many organisations. For example, a senior management team meeting that is always followed by a boozy night out in a lap-dancing club sends out an immediate signal that women are not really welcome. Your right here? To challenge the culture through the courts if you want to – although understandably many women in this situation simply choose to look for another job.

Race discrimination

It is equally unlawful to block someone's job opportunities because they do not belong to a certain ethnic group or because they are a certain colour or nationality.

Disability discrimination

Here the rules are slightly different. It is unlawful to treat a disabled person less favourably, unless an employer can prove that the less favourable treatment is justified.

Example: John A

John A is a wheelchair user. John A is very keen to get a promotion to the Prototype Development Office – a move for which he is well qualified. The only snag for John A is that the Prototype Development Office is on the fifth floor and there is no lift.

Would it be justifiable in this case to turn John A down for promotion on the grounds of his disability? Not straight away. There is a test that his employers have to satisfy to demonstrate that they have not discriminated against him unlawfully. They have to investigate first whether it would be possible to make an adjustment to the job – one that would cater for John A's disability. For example:

- Could they fit a stair lift?
- Could they move the Prototype Development Office to the ground floor?
- Could John A do the prototype development work in a ground floor office, i.e. detached from everyone else?

Once John A's employer has gone through the step of looking at adjustments and ruling them out if they are either impossible or impractical, then they may be in a position to turn him down for promotion on the grounds of his disability. If they fail to follow this approach, however, John A will have a very good case for disability discrimination.

Victimisation, harassment and bullying

Where do you stand if you feel that you are being picked on or singled out for unfair treatment?

Racial harassment
Subjecting you to racial taunts or giving you a hard time because you belong to a particular national or ethnic group is clearly unlawful and would be viewed as race discrimination. This applies irrespective of whether the racial harassment is coming from your bosses or from other employees. If you are forced to quit a job because of racial harassment then you could be looking to bring a claim for constructive dismissal in addition to race discrimination.

Sexual harassment
Though sexual harassment is not an offence in itself, having trust and confidence in your employer to behave correctly is an implied term of your contract. Hence, when accepted codes of conduct are broken (e.g. offensive remarks, unwelcomed sexual advances) it could be argued that the implied term has also been breached.

How does this help you?

- If the behaviour in question was the reason that you had to leave your job then you could be looking at a claim for constructive dismissal
- If the behaviour was to the detriment of one sex and not the other (e.g. the office sex pest makes life a misery for all female staff whereas their male counterparts are unaffected) then it could also constitute sex discrimination

As a mark of good practice many organisations have policies or statements setting out their arrangements for ensuring that harassment or victimisation does not take place. Contained in these statements you will often find guidance on what steps to take if you are the victim of detrimental treatment on the grounds of sex or race. In most cases this will be to raise your complaint with a senior manager.

Note: sexual harassment that involves physical contact could constitute a criminal offence.

Other forms of bullying

But what if you are being subjected to victimisation, harassment or bullying that is not to do with your race or your sex? Where do you stand if you are being given a hard time for some other reason?

Reminder

The Employment Rights Act 1996 protects you if you find that you are being victimised because you tried to bring your employer to task for an infringement of your statutory rights. Let us say that you took your employer to an Employment Tribunal over some matter and then found that you were being singled out unfairly for disciplinary action. You could then go back to the tribunal and ask them to look into your case.

Unfair treatment by your employer could also constitute a breach of trust and confidence – the contractual breach we referred to earlier. If you quit the job because of your employer's conduct, you can seek redress by way of a constructive dismissal claim.

Union membership rights

When you start a new job you could find yourself being asked to join a trade union. Alternatively, you could find that a number of your colleagues have joined a trade union and they want you to do the same. What are your rights in these situations? Do you have to go along with the majority? And if you say no, where do you stand if your colleagues start to give you the cold shoulder?

On the other hand, you could be a member of a trade union and find that you are being singled out for less favourable treatment by your employer. You could realise, for example, that you are being given a smaller pay increase than your non-union colleagues or that you are being targeted for disciplinary action. Where do you stand?

The right to join or not to join
Deciding whether you want to be in a trade union or not is entirely a matter for your conscience and the law protects you whichever way you choose. It is unlawful, for instance, for an employer to put pressure on you to join a trade union. Equally it is unlawful for an employer to subject you to detrimental treatment because you are a member of a union.

The right to a fair hearing

What if you feel that you have been treated unfairly? What, for example, if you have been given warnings that you do not feel you deserve?

Raising grievances
Going back to Monday, you will recall our words of warning about flying off into litigation. We advised you to always use internal channels for resolving grievances first. In most cases this simply involves revisiting your company handbook and checking out how to access the grievance procedure. Failing this, a glance at your written statement of particulars will tell you:

- Who to raise grievances with
- How to go about it
- Subsequent steps to follow, i.e. details of what to do next if you are unhappy with the answer you get

The Government's Arbitration Conciliation and Advisory Service (ACAS) has produced a Code of Practice on Disciplinary and Grievance Procedures which contains guidance for employers. The relevance of all ACAS codes is that, while they are not legally binding, they are taken into account by Employment Tribunals. An employer who has not followed an ACAS code will face an uphill struggle in front of a tribunal.

Grievance procedures

One of the features of the ACAS code is that it encourages employers to develop procedures for dealing with grievances, i.e. stages where increasingly senior levels of management are brought in to try to resolve the differences. In other words, employers who give you a brush off after a quick exchange of words are flaunting the ACAS code. The penalty for your employer will be if the grievance forces you to hand in your notice and go to a tribunal with a complaint of constructive dismissal. Not hearing you out properly will go against them and probably lose them the case.

Collective agreements

Where trade unions are involved in companies, there are often agreed procedures for resolving disputes – including individual grievances.

Appeals against disciplinary action

In your written particulars there will be details of the steps you should follow if you are dissatisfied with any disciplinary decision. If, for instance, you feel that a warning you have been given is unjustified or that your boss took a disciplinary decision without being fully aware of all the facts. Access to appeal against disciplinary decisions is one of your contractual rights.

Human rights

The Human Rights Act 1998 imported parts of the European
Convention on Human Rights into UK law. This had the
effect of introducing an important new dimension to
employment rights.

Strictly speaking, rights under the Human Rights Act
apply only to people employed in public undertakings,
for example, police officers, civil servants, local
government workers. One of the stipulations, however,
is that courts of law such as Employment Tribunals
must take the Convention into account when reaching
their decisions. In other words, the Act has relevance
for everyone.

Employment rights contained in the European Convention
are as follows:

- The right not to be held in slavery or in forced or
  compulsory labour (Article 4)
- The right to respect for private and family life
  including the privacy of employees' homes and
  correspondence (Article 8)
- The right to freedom of thought, conscience and
  religion including the right to religious worship
  (Article 9)
- The right to freedom of expression (Article 10)
- The right to freedom of assembly and association
  (Article 11)
- The right to freedom from discrimination (Article 14)

Article 11 underlines your right to belong or not to belong to a trade union. Article 14 lends further weight to your right not to suffer detrimental treatment at the hands of your employer for discriminatory reasons. Later in the week we will be seeing more examples of where the European Convention gives you extra muscle when it comes to exercising your job rights.

Rights of part-time, temporary and agency workers

Where do you stand, however, if you are part of the fringe workforce? What rights do you have if:

- You only do a few hours a week?
- Your employment is short-term?
- You are employed by an agency?
- You work freelance?

Part-timers

Where you work less hours than the majority of your colleagues, you may be classed as a part-timer. But where does this leave you when it comes to your employment rights? Can your employer treat you any less favourably because you are not a full-time member of staff?

The answer here is a very simple one. Thanks to a European Directive brought into UK law by the Part-time Workers (Prevention of Less Favourable Treatment) Regulations 2000, part-time workers now enjoy the same statutory rights as their full-time counterparts. Furthermore, the regulations cancel out anything in your contract of employment that puts part-timers on a less favourable footing to everyone else. Among other things, this means that your employer can no longer exclude you from benefits such as sick pay and pension schemes. It also means that you cannot be picked for redundancy because you are a part-timer.

Temporary workers

Where do you stand if you are employed as a temp or on a fixed-term contract?

Temps and contract workers have the same statutory rights as everyone else. Note, however, that many statutory rights are subject to a service qualification. For example, the right to receive a statutory redundancy payment is subject to a service qualification of 2 years.

Some (less scrupulous) employers have the habit of rehiring people on a succession of temporary contracts. When the gaps between these temporary contracts are short, an employment tribunal is likely to take the view that they constitute one continuous period of employment. This is important when it comes to assessing your eligibility for service-related statutory rights.

Agency workers

What if you work as a temp but you are employed by an agency, rather than by organisation where you work? How does this affect your rights?

An agency worker is no different to anyone else when it comes to employment rights. Statutes apply to you and you have a contract of employment, except in your case it is with the agency. The agency is your employer if any question of rights should arise.

Freelancers

If you are genuinely self-employed, i.e. a defined business entity accountable to no one except yourself and receiving money by sending out invoices to your clients, then most of what is in this book is not relevant to you. Watch out, though, for the following:

- Where employers engage staff on a 'self-employed basis' for no reason other than to avoid employment rights. Put to the test, you could find an Employment Tribunal taking an entirely different view and deciding that an employment relationship does exist
- Some employment law talks about 'workers' rather than 'employees' (The Working Time Regulations are an example). 'Workers' has a rather broader definition and could include a service provider

Summary

You have a right to fair treatment and you cannot be given the rough end of the stick:

- Because of your gender
- Because you belong to a particular religious, national or ethnic group
- For reasons of disabilities
- Because you belong or refuse to belong to a trade union
- Because you work part-time or because you are engaged on a temporary or fixed-term contract

In some cases, the rights you have to fair treatment are backed by EU law giving yet more power to your elbow.

The right to a life

Today we are going to consider what rights you have to a work–life balance. Your list of subjects is as follows:

- Working time – the rights you have when your job involves long hours
- Getting away from it – the right to take time off
- Time off for family
- The right to privacy

Working time

We are not all workaholics and most of us subscribe to the view that a balanced life makes for a fitter, better and more rounded person. But where do you stand if you are under pressure from your employer to work long hours? What rights do you have to say enough is enough?

Limits on weekly working hours

With the exception of people like doctors, police officers and transport workers (who have their own hours rules), European law gives you the right to work no more than 48 hours a week (taken on average). In the UK, this right is contained in the Working Time Regulations which became law in 1998.

Opt outs

However, what if you are happy to work long hours? Then a further right you have under the Regulations is to opt out of the 48-hour week rule by giving your employer a signed agreement. You may be inclined to sign an opt-out if, for example, your household budget is geared to the amount of money you can earn from working overtime.

Where you determine your own hours

If you are a manager, you may be in a position where you determine your own hours. In this case, the regulations may not apply to you and striking the balance between life and work is something that you have to sort out for yourself.

What your contract has to say

Your company handbook could contain information on how your employer applies the 48-hour rule, including:

- Arrangements for recording working time
- Details of the periods over which working time is averaged
- Whether you are under compulsion to work additional hours, for example, to help your employer meet surges in demand

Do not jump to the conclusion that your employer is in breach of the Working Time Regulations just because you happen to work more than 48 hours in one particular week. What you need to look at is the average hours you work over a period. Normally this period is 17 weeks but you employer may be subject to special circumstances – which is why it is advisable to check your contract first.

Collective and workforce agreements
Employers have some flexibility in the way that they implement the Regulations. They can, for example, come to an agreement with a trade union or with employee representatives on detailed arrangements. Where there is such an agreement, you need to look at it carefully to understand your rights fully.

Health and safety
Working long hours can have a detrimental effect on your health. Furthermore, excessive tiredness can cause loss of concentration and make you more prone to accidents. The point here is that, as we shall see tomorrow, you have a right in law to say no to anything that puts your health and safety at risk. So, even though your employer may not be in breach of the Working Time Regulations technically, you may still have right on your side if the hours you are being asked to work are excessive.

11 hours' rest
Quite separately, the Working Time Regulations give you an entitlement to take 11 hours' rest in every 24-hour period. This puts a further limit on the number of hours that you can be asked to work in a day.

Note: if you are under 18 you have a right to 12 hours' rest.

Getting away from it

What rights do you have to your weekends or to a few days off when you have been working continuously over a period?

Weekly rest
Other than the provisions for daily rest, the Working Time Regulations also give you the right to at least 24 hours off in every 7-day period. In the case of under-18s this right extends to 48 hours.

> You also have the right, under the Working Time Regulations, to 4 weeks paid holiday a year. You will recall that we looked at the right to paid holiday on Tuesday.

Check your contract
Some employers provide for time away from the job in the form of:

- Study leave for those preparing to take examinations
- Time off for overseas travel
- Provision for career breaks
- Time off to attend special events such as religious festivals
- In the case of those whose roots are in other countries, leave of absence to 'go back home'

The above are just examples of the kind of arrangements

employers have to make their conditions of employment more attractive. In short, with time away from the job, it is not unusual to find that you have contractual entitlements that far exceed any rights given to you under statute law. Therefore, check your company handbook and/or conditions of employment carefully.

Time off for family

What rights do you have when:

- You have to visit an antenatal clinic?
- You stop work to have a baby?
- You are a father?
- You want to return to your job?
- You want to take time off for the care of young children?
- You are needed at home to look after someone who depends on you?

Needing antenatal care
If you are pregnant and your doctor or other health care professional refers you to an antenatal clinic, you have a right to take time off with pay. Your employer may want you to produce:

- Evidence you are pregnant (e.g. a medical certificate)
- Your appointment card

Maternity leave
Every woman has a statutory right to take maternity leave in
the period before and after her baby is born. In addition,
there are an increasing number of employers who have
'family friendly' policies where entitlements go far beyond
the statutory requirement.

Paternity leave
From 2003, fathers will have a statutory right to 2 weeks'
paternity leave in the 8-week period following the birth of
their child. Again, there are 'family friendly' employers with
more generous entitlements.

Returning to work after maternity
You have a right to return to your old job after maternity
leave. Your employer is allowed to cover for your absence by,
for example, hiring a temp, but this must not interfere with
you exercising your right to return. Any detrimental
treatment you receive because you have taken maternity
leave is also unlawful.

Parental leave
If you are a parent with very young children you may feel it
important to take some time away from the job to be with
them – or to be at home to help with the domestic chores.

The European Parental Leave Directive gives every parent
with a child under five the right to a total of 13 weeks'
unpaid leave. They can take this leave:

- Spread over 5 years
- Any time after they have clocked up 12 months'
  service with their employer

Many employers have their own parental leave schemes, hence it is advisable to check your company handbook and/or conditions of employment to establish the full extent of your rights. Conversely, there could be a collective or workforce agreement that covers your employer's parental leave arrangements.

Taking time off to care for dependants
What happens if your children are sick and there is no one else to look after them? What happens if some other domestic emergency crops up which causes you to be absent from work?

The law allows you to take a 'reasonable' amount of unpaid time off to deal with family crises – particularly where care of a dependant, such as a child is involved. To exercise this right you must:

- Tell your employer what is going on as soon as possible
- Give your employer an idea of how long you are going to be away

This right to time off for care of dependants also extends to a death in the family.

The right to privacy

At work, what protection do you have against intrusion into your privacy? How far can your employer legitimately go when it comes to keeping tabs on you and what rights do you have when you feel that they are overstepping the mark?

Reminder

Article 8 of the European Convention on Human Rights gives everyone the right to privacy in respect of their home, family and correspondence.

Private telephone calls
What are your rights when it comes to monitoring your telephone calls?

Whether you have a right to make and receive private telephone calls is a matter for your contract of employment. Here, you may find that your employer has written rules about the use of telephones or it may be left to custom and practice on the part of the organisation where you work, i.e. an implied contractual term. Where problems do arise, however, is where employers monitor telephone traffic as a matter of routine, for example, to check that standards of customer service are being maintained. Where do you stand if you suspect your private conversations are being eavesdropped or recorded? Have you the right to object?

Under European law, your employer should tell you if your phone calls are being monitored and a failure to do so may amount to an infringement of your human rights. If the monitoring involves recording (i.e. tapes or transcriptions of tapes that are stored on file) then you have additional rights under Data Protection legislation (rights that we will be looking at shortly).

The same rules apply if e-mails and internet usage are being monitored. Nevertheless, many employers now have internet and e-mail policies setting out what is expected of staff and where disciplinary sanctions could be used.

Surveillance
Although it is unlikely that you will ever find that your office has been bugged, surveillance is routinely carried out by many organisations as part of their security. CCTV cameras is one form of surveillance that we are all familiar with.

Surveillance as a deterrent to crime is clearly in everyone's best interests, but is there a point where surveillance becomes intrusive and potentially sinister? What if you really do feel that Big Brother is watching you? Where can you draw the line?

Implied in everyone's contract of employment is an obligation of trust and confidence that works both ways. So, just as it is up to you not to do anything that would break this obligation (e.g. leak confidential information to a competitor), it is equally up to your employer not to do the same. Oppressive surveillance measures such as CCTV or hidden recording devices in areas where employees could reasonably expect to have some privacy (e.g. rest rooms and lavatories) could be viewed as a breach of trust and confidence – particularly where there is little or no justification. This would come into play if, for example:

- The surveillance led to your dismissal (the contractual breach could be used to substantiate a claim of unfair dismissal)
- Surveillance became the reason for you quitting (you could bring a claim of constructive dismissal)

Where surveillance, such as CCTV, is in use then your employer should bring this to your attention, for example, by putting up a sign. Where surveillance recordings are made and kept on file again,you have further rights under Data Protection Law (more on this in a moment)

Private property
You may not like the idea of a manager or a security officer going through the drawers of your desk or rummaging in your briefcase. But where do you stand if your employer insists on searching your personal belongings? What rights do you have when you feel that interference with your private property is taken too far?

Employers have a right to protect their businesses particularly where:

- Pilfering or other criminal acts are a problem, for example, where high value materials are stored on the premises
- A high level of security is needed for other reasons, for example, the work is secret

To this end, employers may insert the right to search personal property in their company handbooks and/or conditions of employment. At the start of your employment they may even ask you to sign a form to give your consent.

Irrespective of whether you have previously consented or not, a search that involves any kind of bodily contact is likely to constitute a criminal assault – meaning that you have every right to refuse (or call the police if the search proceeds). Similarly, a search that results in damage to your property (e.g. damage to your car) is also a criminal act.

In general, you have a right to say no to requests to search personal items such as handbags and briefcases. However, when the property in question belongs to your employer rather than to you (e.g. your workstation or your company car) then you are on more shaky ground. Nevertheless, you could seek compensation for any loss or damage to your property that results from such a search, for example, a box of CDs that goes missing after the search of your company car.

What employers have no right to do is impound property that belongs to you. Ask for it back and, if nothing happens, you can complain to the police.

Note also that:

- A search carried out in a manner that is offensive or degrading could constitute a contractual breach
- Saying no to a search could leave a suspicious employer with no option other than to summon the police, i.e. be aware of the possible consequences of exercising your rights

Accessing information on file
What is the position if you have reason to believe that your employer is keeping secret files on you? How can you find out:

- What is on the files?
- What use it is being put to?
- Who has access to it?

Under data protection law, you have the right to put these questions to your employer in writing and to receive a reply within 40 days. If you are still not satisfied, you can ask for a copy of the information that is being stored on file so that you can see for yourself what it contains. This applies both to information stored electronically (on disc) or on paper-based systems.

> Note: there are some circumstances where your employer is entitled to refuse you access to the files – for example, when another person is named (someone who has not consented to the release of the information to you) or where the outcome of a criminal investigation could be prejudiced.

Challenging an employer's right to hold information on file
As we have seen already, the law recognises that some information held on employer's files is 'sensitive'. For example, information about your medical history or about your sex life. Bearing in mind that such information could come from several different sources (including taped telephone conversations), you may not be too happy to find that your employer has retained it. What can you do?

> • First, if the sensitive information has been gathered without your consent you can challenge it on this basis alone
> • Second, if the information dates from a long time ago and is not relevant to anything happening currently, you can challenge your employer's right to retain it

Other than sensitive information, you can ask your employer to remove anything from your file that:

- Could cause you damage or distress
- Is inaccurate or misleading

Summary

Today we have looked at your rights when it comes to:

- Having a life outside work
- Having time with your family
- Preventing intrusion into your privacy

Many disputes in employment are over the right to a life, therefore it is important to know where you stand.

Looking after your health and safety

You have important rights when it comes to your health and safety and this is the subject we will be looking at next. The list of topics is as follows:

- Employers' duties – statutory duties and the duty of care
- Providing you with a safe and healthy working environment
- Safe working practices and the assessment of risk
- Health care and access to medical facilities

Employers' duties

What rights do you have when it comes to your personal well-being? With health and safety, what protection should your employer provide?

The duty of care
A long-established principle in UK law, is the duty of care – a duty owed by all employers to the people who work for them. The duty of care is an implied term in every contract of employment and this means that an employer who fails to exercise care is automatically committing a contractual breach.

Statutory duties
However, in addition to the duty of care, there is also a substantial body of legislation governing workplace health and safety. Chief among this legislation is the 1974 Health &

Safety at Work Act ,which places a general duty on all employers to look after the health and safety of their employees – a duty that is echoed in European law.

Your rights need to be seen against this background of employers' duties. In short you have a right to expect employers to discharge their duties and the law is on your side if and when they fail.

Enforcement
Enforcement of health and safety legislation is normally left to the Government's Health & Safety Executive through its various inspectorates, for example, the Factory Inspectorate. Offices and warehouses, however, fall within the control of environmental health departments of local councils.

Negligence
Quite separate to health and safety legislation, you also have the right to sue your employer for negligence. For example, if you fall and break your ankle because the floor was slippery, you can sue for compensation for your losses (including your loss of earnings).

Providing you with a safe and healthy workplace

But where do you stand if your working environment is dangerous and poses risks? What right do you have to get it rectified?

Your employer's duties
The Health & Safety at Work Act puts a specific duty on employers to provide a safe and health working environment. Regulations made under the Act lay down more detailed requirements, for example:

- Effective maintenance so that premises, equipment and machinery are not left in a dangerous state
- Adequate ventilation
- The need for workplaces to be kept at a comfortable temperature
- Adequate lighting
- A good standard of cleanliness
- Adequate space for people to work
- Workstations that are comfortable and suitable seating to be provided
- Floors, stairs and aisles to be kept clear and free of clutter
- Properly marked routes for trucks and cars

- Special attention to the possibility of injury from falls (or from falling objects)
- Windows and glass doors to be either shielded or made of sufficiently strong material to prevent people who fall into them receiving injuries from cuts
- Equipment, such as poles, to be provided when opening a window, ventilator or skylight that would otherwise be difficult
- Window cleaning to be carried out without exposing anyone to risk of injury
- Doors to be properly fitted and maintained
- Escalators (where used) to function safely
- Adequate lavatory arrangements for the number of staff employed – these to be properly ventilated and kept in a good state of cleanliness with separate accommodation for males and females
- Adequate washing facilities
- Access to drinking water
- Somewhere for staff to keep their clothes
- Facilities for changing (where this is a requirement of the job)

Protecting you from fire

Under fire protection regulations, your employer is required to provide:

- Adequate fire-fighting equipment (e.g. extinguishers)
- Fire detectors and alarms
- Escape routes and emergency exits (properly signed)
- Nominated persons trained to take charge in the event of a fire

Protecting you from electrical hazards
Electrical equipment in workplaces is potentially dangerous
and your employer has duties to ensure that:

- Equipment is sited so that it does not pose risks –
  this includes siting power points so that cables are
  not trailing across gangways
- Plugs and other connecting devices are correctly
  specified
- Equipment is properly maintained

Protecting you from hazardous substances
Where your employer's business involves the use of hazardous
substances (e.g. toxic chemicals) then there is a duty to:

- Carry out a proper risk assessment to determine the
  extent of any hazards and the steps that need to be
  taken to protect employees

- Minimise your exposure to the substance by, for example, providing you with the correct protective equipment
- Provide you with the necessary training

Where you are at risk of exposure to hazardous substances you have the right to medical check ups and paid time off to attend. You also have a right to see any medical information on you that is kept on file. This right is separate to the right to access files under Data Protection legislation referred to on Thursday.

Protecting you from tobacco smoke
Smoking is an emotive issue but, if you are a non-smoker, what right do you have to work in a tobacco-free environment? Indeed, can you protest when people around you start to light up?

In addition to the requirement to provide rest areas and areas for the consumption of food, employers also have to provide

a place where employees can take their breaks or eat their meals, free from the annoyance of tobacco smoke. Other than this there is no statutory duty on employers to segregate smokers from non-smokers. However, in practice many organisations have introduced strict rules about smoking, so the right to breathe tobacco-free air is one that you could find you have through your contract of employment.

Living with VDUs

In an age where business is driven by information technology, most of us spend some of our working day sitting in front of a screen. There are, however, some health risks attached to too much VDU use, notably:

- Musculo-skeletal disorders arising from poor posture and/or workstation design
- Tiredness
- Eyestrain

So what rights do you have if using a VDU forms a significant part of your daily routine?

- Your workstation (the equipment you use, your seat and your immediate surroundings) must meet certain minimum requirements and, to this effect, your employer must carry out an assessment of whether it is up to scratch or not. Where, for example, a chair is found to be defective, it must be repaired or replaced
- You have a right to take a break or to have a change of activity if your work involves sitting in front of a screen for long periods

- If you request it, you have the right to have an eye test (your employer must foot the bill)
- If the eye test shows that you need glasses for VDU work, you have the right to a pair at your employer's expense
- You have the right to be given proper training

Note: the above rights will not apply to you if you only use a VDU occasionally.

Protecting you from noise
Exposure to high levels of noise can:

- Damage your hearing
- Affect your concentration
- Make communication difficult

So what if your workplace is noisy? What rights do you have to protection from exposure?

Where there is concern about noise, employers are required to carry out monitoring to determine:

- Its level
- The possible effects of exposure

If you are going to be exposed to excessive and potentially harmful noise you have a right to be told. If your employer is unable to eliminate or reduce the noise (i.e. you continue to be exposed) you have a further right to be provided with suitable ear protection.

Safe working practices

What rights do you have to ensure that you are provided with everything you need to carry out your tasks, in a manner that will not be detrimental to your health and safety?

Giving you information
Clearly, you need to know if there are any risks associated with your job and the steps that you need to take to keep them to a minimum. How do you find out?

Under European and UK law, your employer must carry out a *risk assessment* identifying any potential dangers that arise from the activities of the business.

You have a right to know:

- The nature of the dangers
- What you need to do to protect yourself
- If any of the dangers are serious, for example, life threatening
- Procedures to follow in an emergency
- Who is responsible

- If you are a woman of child-bearing age, any risks to you or your child if you should become pregnant

Note: if you work at home your employer still has a duty to carry out a risk assessment, for instance, on the room in your house that you use as an office.

Providing you with training
You have a right to be provided with any training that you need in order to do your job without risk of personal injury or damage to your health. Training should be given to you:

- When you start in your job
- When a risk arises that was not there previously, for example, from the introduction of a new process or method of working

Providing you with protective equipment
You have a right to be provided with any protective equipment needed to reduce your exposure to risk. For example, a hard hat if your work involves paying visits to construction sites or safety footwear if you are at risk from heavy objects dropping on to your toes. Your employer also has a duty to ensure that the protective equipment:

- Is capable of doing the job
- Fits you properly
- Complies with any statutory rules concerning its design and manufacture, i.e. that it is tested to a specified standard
- Is replaced as and when needed

Note: your employer also has a duty to ensure that you know how to use the protective equipment and that it is practical and comfortable to wear.

Health care and access to medical facilities

What rights do you have to a medical check up every now and then? What facilities should your employer provide when it comes to looking after your physical well-being?

Where medical check-ups are prescribed by law
We have touched already on situations where employers are required by law to carry out systematic health monitoring. For example:

- Where there is a risk of exposure to hazardous substances
- Ear tests where there is a risk of exposure to high levels of noise

We have also seen that people who use display screen equipment on a regular basis can ask to have their eyes tested.

In addition to these statutory requirements, there are regulations in force in certain industries (e.g. asbestos) calling for employers to provide regular health checks.

Note: if you are asked to work nights you can ask for:

- A medical check up before you start
- Further checks ups from time to time

First aid

Given that most accidents at work are fairly minor, what right do you have to receive first-aid treatment?

Every employer, irrespective of size, must provide a proper first-aid box or – where larger numbers of people are employed – adequate first-aid facilities to take account of their numbers, dispersal and working arrangements, i.e. shift rotas.

You should also be provided with a basic first-aid box if you work from home or if your work involves travel (e.g. one that you can keep in your car).

If you work in a large establishment or one where special hazards are present, your employer may be required to provide a properly equipped first-aid room or a surgery with appropriate staffing (e.g. a qualified nurse).

Other than this all employers are required to have sufficient competent and trained first-aid personnel.

Summary

You have a right to be protected against any health and safety hazards that could arise from carrying out your day-to-day functions. In particular your employer must ensure that you are:

- Trained properly
- Advised of any risks
- Cared for and protected from exposure to those risks

At the end

Today is the last day of your short course in employment
rights. Appropriately, we are going to look at what happens
when employment ends – or threatens to. The list of topics
looks like this:

- Taken over, sold off or merged – your rights when
  the identity of your employer changes
- Ceased trading or gone broke – where you stand
  when your employer's business fails
- Facing redundancy – what happens when your
  services are no longer required
- Dismissal on health grounds
- Where your conduct or performance is the issue
- Rights after you have left employment

Business transfers

Businesses change hands – sometimes with alarming
regularity. But where do you stand if your firm forms part of
a merger or is taken over by someone else? What are your
rights if new owners come along and start making changes
or, worse still, threaten you with the sack?

Transfer or not
Let us take two examples:

Example A

Boggis & Co, widget-makers, was previously a wholly-owned subsidiary of the Clueless & Cumbersome Group. Clueless & Cumbersome found, however, that they could not make an adequate return from widget-making and so they sold Boggis & Co to its biggest rival – Smartfast International Widgets.

Example B

Oddballs Plastic Oddments previously had a department making oddments with left-handed threads. Oddballs decided, however, to pull out of the market for non-standard products and sold the department to a consortium made up of its management team.

In Example A, the business (Boggis & Co) continued to exist, albeit with different parentage. Each contract of employment was still therefore between Boggis & Co and the individual employee. In short, each employee's contractual position was unaffected by the sale of the business and any rights they had were carried forward.

In Example B, however, employees of the left-handed thread department originally had their contracts with Oddballs Plastic Oddments and this is no longer the case. They are now employed by the new consortium. In short, their contracts have been transferred. The identity of their employer has changed.

> Employees in transferred businesses are protected by the law. With the exception of occupational pensions, they have the right to continuity of employment and to the terms and conditions that they enjoyed previously. So, for instance, if the consortium in Example B tried to force its own (less favourable) conditions, they would be committing a contractual breach. This would leave them wide open to claims of constructive dismissal if employees of the left-hand thread department decided to vote with their feet and quit.

Dismissal arising from a transfer
What happens if the new owners of a business decides to dismiss some of the existing staff? What happens if the new owners want to slim down the business or to put some of their own people into the key positions?

To dismiss someone simply because of a business transfer is automatically unfair and, if you are ever in this position, you can go to an Employment Tribunal and ask for compensation. Where there is a genuine need for less people (i.e. a redundancy situation) then your new employer is required to inform you and give you the reasons. Genuine, in this context, means a genuine economic, organisational or technical reason, rather than your face not fitting (or someone else's face being preferred).

> The new owners would have to satisfy the tribunal that their reasons were genuine and the onus of proof would rest on them.

Your rights if your employer goes out of business

What happens if your employer is insolvent? What rights do you have:

> • Generally?
> • To any money that you are owed?

Terminating your contract
It does not follow that your contract of employment terminates because your employer is insolvent. The business can carry on trading, for example, to enable a suitable buyer to be found. Somewhere along the line, though, the shedding of staff is almost inevitable – whether it arises from liquidation of the business and its assets or it comes about as part of a general move to cut costs. Where do you stand if you lose your job through your employer's insolvency? The short answer is that you are redundant and you qualify for any entitlements that arise from this fact. Notably you are entitled to:

- Consultation
- Proper notice
- Redundancy pay

Note: redundancy is the subject we will be looking at next.

Where money is owed to you
In the weeks leading up to insolvency, it is not uncommon to find that employees have not been paid or have not been paid in full because of their employer's shortage of funds. What rights do you have to get back any money that you are owed by an insolvent employer?

Under UK law (The Insolvency Act 1986) wages owed to employees come under the heading of a preferential debt meaning that you can jump the queue when it comes to paying off other creditors such as suppliers.

There is no guarantee, however, that there will be sufficient funds to meet your claim for unpaid wages. Nevertheless, once your employment is terminated you can claim for at least part of the money to be paid out of the National Insurance Fund. By this stage, money owing could include redundancy pay.

Facing redundancy

Sadly, being made redundant is something that most of us are going to experience at least once in our working lives. Where do you stand and what are your rights when your employer decides that your services are no longer required?

Giving you the facts
Can the boss call you into the office and hand you a brown envelope containing your notice or are you entitled to receive some prior warning that your name could appear on a redundancy list?

Where your employer is contemplating 20 or more redundancies within a 90-day period there is a requirement in law to consult with:

- *Either* the recognised trade union
- *Or* representatives chosen by employees

This consultation must begin at least 30 days before the first dismissals are due to take place. Your employer must tell representatives:

- Why there is a need for redundancies
- Who will be affected (where the axe will fall)
- How many employees will lose their jobs
- When the redundancies will take place
- Details of any special payments (how they will be calculated)

Where more than 100 employees are at risk of redundancy, this consultation process must begin at least 90 days before the first dismissals are due.

Consultation is about seeking ways of avoiding redundancies (or minimising their impact). Your employer must enter into meaningful discussions with your representatives with these aims in mind. Chief among the topics for discussion will be the availability of alternative employment (other jobs that you can do and which can be offered to you).

Case law has established that consultation must also extend to individuals. In short, if you are not among a batch of 20 plus redundancies, you still have a right to be told if your job is at risk.

Giving you notice

Given that there is nothing your employer can do to avoid making you redundant, you have a right to be given the correct period of notice. 'Correct' means whichever is the longest:

- *Either* your contractual period of notice
- *Or* the minimum period of notice laid down in the Employment Rights Act (i.e. providing you have been employed for over 1 month, 1 week's notice per year of service – up to a maximum of 12)

Having time off to look for another job

During your notice period you have a right to a reasonable amount of time off, with pay, for job-hunting purposes. Your employer may ask you to produce proof that you are using the time legitimately (e.g. sight of a letter inviting you to attend an interview).

Your right to redundancy pay

If you have more than 2 years' service, you have a right to a minimum statutory redundancy payment. How much you get depends on:

- Your age
- Your length of service

What you may find, however, is that your employer makes payments to redundant employees that exceed the state scheme, i.e. a contractual arrangement.

Note: redundancy or severance payment schemes are often contained in collective agreements.

Dismissing you on health grounds

What rights do you have when your health is the reason for you losing your job? What happens when, through long absence or the onset of a major illness, your employer decides your employment can no longer be continued.

Medical evidence
Before taking the drastic step of terminating your employment on health grounds, your employer may want to seek the advice of a medical practitioner and this could mean your own doctor or one that your employer nominates.

On Sunday we looked at the right you have to be given first sight of any pre-employment medical reports and, if necessary, to challenge their contents. This right extends to medical reports that your employer asks for during the course of your employment – including reports that could indicate you are no longer fit to do your job.

Examining all the alternatives
Given that your health has broken down to such an extent that you are unable to continue in your job, your condition will probably fall under the heading of a disability within the

meaning of the Disability Discrimination Act. This automatically places a duty on your employer to see:

- Whether your job could be adjusted in any way (to enable your employment to continue)
- Whether any alternative work could be found for you (work that would be within your capabilities)

If your employer dismisses you without considering adjustments and alternatives, you would be in a position to claim compensation for disability discrimination.

Performance and conduct issues

What if your misbehaviour or your failure to come up to standard is the reason that you are being threatened with the sack? What rights do you have when faced with disciplinary action?

The right to fair warning

There is no law forcing employers to have formal disciplinary procedures but those that do not face an uphill struggle when it comes to defending unfair dismissal claims before an Employment Tribunal. The chances are, therefore, that your employer has a disciplinary procedure and that, contained in this procedure, is your right to have fair warning if your continued misbehaviour or performance could lead to you having the sack.

The right to be accompanied

Under the Employment Relations Act 1999, you have a right to be accompanied by a colleague at any disciplinary meetings. If you are a union member you could elect to be accompanied by your union representative (or by a full-time union official). The presence of a colleague is helpful, not just for moral support, but also as a witness to anything that is said.

The right to appeal

If you are given a warning or dismissed, what right do you have to appeal? What if you think the boss has got it in for you and a more impartial mind would see things differently?

Your statement of written particulars (see Monday) tells you who you can appeal to if you are dissatisfied with any disciplinary decision. This is the route to follow if you are unhappy with the treatment that you have received. In addition, your employer's disciplinary procedure may contain information on what steps to take if you wish to make an appeal.

Rights once you have finished

What rights do you have after you have left a job?

The right to claim unfair dismissal
If you are unhappy with the way your employment has ended then you have a right to claim unfair dismissal – a right that we have touched upon a number of times during the course of this week. This means that you could put your case to an Employment Tribunal and ask them to decide whether your employer treated you reasonably or not.

Do not forget that constructive dismissal is a form of unfair dismissal – when you left the job because of your employer's conduct; when you felt that you had no alternative other than to resign.

To claim unfair dismissal you must:

- Have 12 months' service
- Register your claim within 3 months of your employment ending

Note: where the reason for leaving was linked to a race, gender or disabilities issue, you have a separate right to enter a claim for discrimination. Here the service qualification does not apply. You can make a discrimination claim irrespective of how long you have been with your employer.

The right to a fair reference
We looked at your right to be given a fair reference on Sunday. Your employer is not entitled to say anything about you that is either untrue or misleading.

Looking back over the week

In the world we live in today, you are increasingly on your own when it comes to fighting your corner against employers who are either unscrupulous, ignorant or who, in their hurry to get things done, forget to take individuals' rights into account. This is why it is more important than ever to know where you stand when it comes to dealing with the wide range of issues that can arise in the course of employment. Hopefully the lessons of the last 7 days will help you in this respect. More importantly, you should view your knowledge of employment rights as central to the job of managing your own career successfully and of being prepared for all eventualities. Remember that new rights are coming along all the time and so it is vital to keep yourself up to date.

Further information

Arbitration Conciliation and Advisory Service
ACAS
Head Office
Brandon House
180 Borough High Street
London
SE1 1LW
Telephone: 020 7210 3613
http://www.acas.org.uk

Citizens Advice Bureaux
Myddelton House
115–123 Pentonville Road
London N1 9LZ
Telephone: 020 7833 2181
http://www.nacab.org.uk

Commission for Racial Equality
CRE
Elliot House
10–12 Allington Street
London SW1E 5EH
Tel: 020 7828 7022
Fax: 020 7630 7605
E-mail: info@cre.gov.uk
http://www.cre.gov.uk

Equal Opportunities Commission
Customer Contact Point
Equal Opportunities Commission
Arndale House
Arndale Centre
Manchester
M4 3EQ
Tel: 08456 015901
Fax: 0161 838 8312
E-mail: info@eoc.org.uk
http://www.eoc.org.uk

Disability Rights Commission
DRC Helpline
Freepost MID 02164
Stratford-upon-Avon
CV37 9BR
Tel: 08457 622 633
Fax: 08457 622 644
Textphone: 08457 622 644
E-mail: ddahelp@stra.sitel.co.uk
http://www.drc.org.uk